France

Written by

Lionel Bender

Consultant Madéline Samuels

Illustrated by

Ann Savage

SILVER BURDETT PRESS
MORRISTOWN, NEW JERSEY

Editor Steve Parker
Editor, U.S. Edition Joanne Fink
Designer Patrick Nugent
Photo-researcher Hugh Olliff
Studio services Kenneth Ward

A TEMPLAR BOOK

Devised and produced by Templar Publishing Ltd
107 High Street, Dorking, Surrey, England, RH4 1QA

Adapted and first published in the United States
in 1988 by Silver Burdett Press, Morristown, N.J.

Color separations by Positive Colour Ltd, Maldon, Essex, England
Printed by L.E.G.O., Vicenza, Italy

Library of Congress Cataloging-in-Publication Data

Bender, Lionel.
  France / written by Lionel Bender : illustrated by Ann Savage.
    p.   cm. — (People and places)
  "A Templar book" — T.p. verso
  Includes index
  Summary: Text and pictures introduce the history, geography,
people, and culture of France.
  ISBN 0-382-09505-7
1. France—Juvenile literature.   [1. France.]   I. Savage, Ann.
ill.   II. Title.   III. Series: People and places (Morristown, N.J.)
DC17.B44 1988
944—dc19   87-22946
                                           CIP
                                            AC

Contents

AT THE CROSSROADS

France lies at the very heart of Europe. It stretches 625 miles from north to south and about the same east to west. It is the largest country in Western Europe. It has borders with six other countries, while Britain, Northern Europe and the Mediterranean countries are only short sea journeys away. More than 3,000 years ago the Celts, from central Europe, recognized this. They soon settled in France and began to enjoy the warm climate and the many crops that could be grown in the rich soil.

In recent times the country has gone from strength to strength. The French are now the largest producers and exporters of agricultural goods in Europe. France is a leading member of the United Nations, the Council of Europe, and the European Economic Community (the EEC or "Common Market").

KEY FACTS

▶ France's land area is 210,040 square miles – four-fifths the size of the state of Texas.
▶ Nearly 55 million people live there.
▶ The capital and biggest city is Paris, with a population of two and a half million in its center.
▶ The official language is French, which is also spoken in neighboring Switzerland, Luxembourg, and Belgium.
▶ The main religion is Roman Catholic.
▶ The unit of money is the *franc* (F or f). One franc is divided into 100 *centimes* (c).

Symbols of France

The red and blue on the "tricolor" (the French flag) are the colors of Paris. In between is white, for royalty. This design was adopted before the French revolution!

The Eiffel Tower in Paris is 984 feet tall. It was built for the 1889 International Exposition and was named after its engineer, Alexandre Eiffel.

6

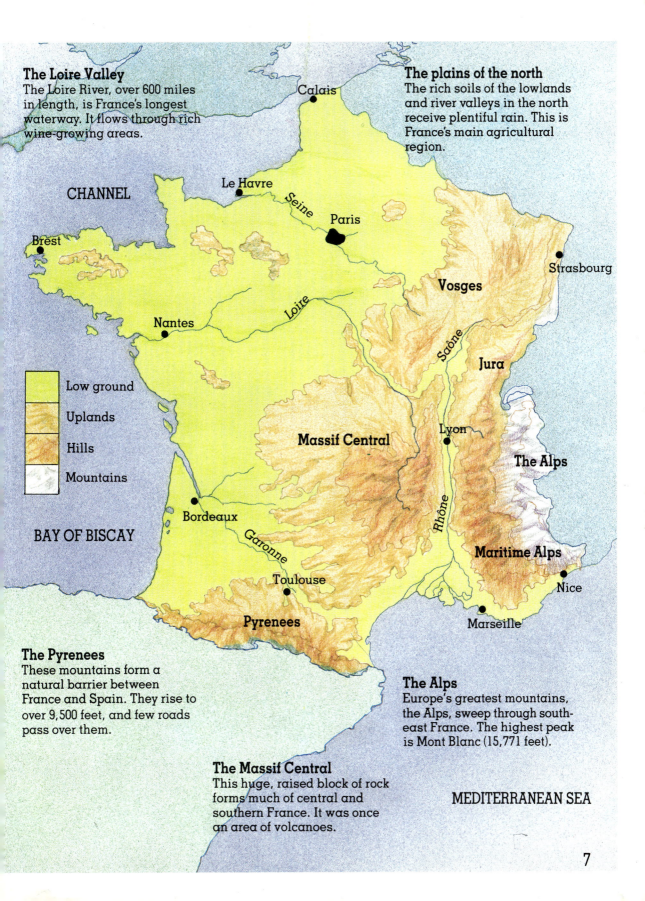

The Loire Valley
The Loire River, over 600 miles in length, is France's longest waterway. It flows through rich wine-growing areas.

The plains of the north
The rich soils of the lowlands and river valleys in the north receive plentiful rain. This is France's main agricultural region.

Calais

CHANNEL

Le Havre

Seine

Paris

Brest

Strasbourg

Vosges

Loire

Nantes

Saône

Jura

Low ground

Uplands

Hills

Mountains

Lyon

Massif Central

The Alps

Bordeaux

Rhône

Maritime Alps

BAY OF BISCAY

Garonne

Toulouse

Nice

Pyrenees

Marseille

The Pyrenees
These mountains form a natural barrier between France and Spain. They rise to over 9,500 feet, and few roads pass over them.

The Alps
Europe's greatest mountains, the Alps, sweep through south-east France. The highest peak is Mont Blanc (15,771 feet).

The Massif Central
This huge, raised block of rock forms much of central and southern France. It was once an area of volcanoes.

MEDITERRANEAN SEA

7

JE SUIS FRANCAIS!

The French language is one of the most important in the world. Many international signs at air and sea ports are in French, and it is the official language of diplomats from every country. But the French people themselves are a mixture of different groups, each with its own customs and language.

The Bretons of Britanny, in the northwest, are descended from the Gauls, a Celtic people. They are hardy folk, eager to preserve their ancient traditions. Many speak their own language, *Breton*, as well as standard French. In the south the Provençaux people are proud of their historical and cultural links with the Roman Empire. They also have their own language, *Langue d'oc*. They speak standard French with a musical lilt and it is said: "They have the sun in their voice."

The Basques live in the southwest corner of France and also in northern Spain. Their origins are a mystery. So is their language, *Eskura*, which has little in common with either French or Spanish.

Names and numbers

France is divided into 96 areas called *départements*. Each *département* has a number which is used in postal codes and car registration numbers. This Renault (a French-made car) is from Seine-Maritime in Normandy.

New arrivals

In this century almost three million foreign people have come to live in France, mostly in the big cities. Many have come from the old French colonies of Algeria, Morocco, and Tunisia. Immigrant workers have come from Spain, Portugal, and Italy.

Breton

Langue d'oc

Basque

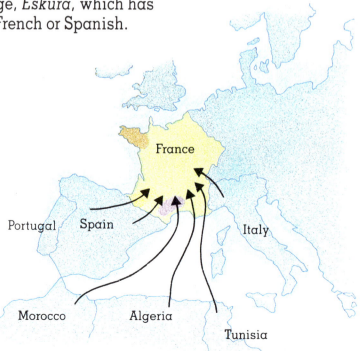

Up, up and away

Joseph and Jacques Montgolfier invented the first hot-air balloon. In 1783 François de Rozier and the Marquis d'Alrandes were the first people to fly. They crossed over Paris in a Montgolfier balloon.

A first in medicine

Louis Pasteur, a French chemist, discovered that many diseases were caused by germs. In 1888 he became the first director of the Pasteur Institute in Paris.

The first movies

In 1895 in Paris, the world's first motion picture audience saw a film made by the Lumière brothers, Louis and Auguste. The brothers invented the *Cinématographe*, a combined camera and projector.

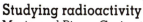

Studying radioactivity

Marie and Pierre Curie studied radioactivity and X-rays, and they discovered the substances radium and polonium. Marie won two Nobel Prizes, in physics (1904) and chemistry (1911).

COUNTRYSIDE AND CLIMATE

France lies almost midway between the Equator and the North Pole, at the same level as southern Canada and the southern Soviet Union. So you might expect the weather to be mild, with cool winters and warm summers. But across the country, the weather is very varied. Some parts are cool and wet, others are hot and dry. This is because of the mountain ranges in the south and east, and also the warm waters of the Gulf Stream that flow in from the Atlantic.

Much of central France has seasonal weather like northeastern America or southern Britain. The winters are cool and the summers are warm, and most rain falls in summer. The farther east you go, the more different the seasons become. There is much snow in winter, and in summer the days are hot and sunny with frequent thunderstorms.

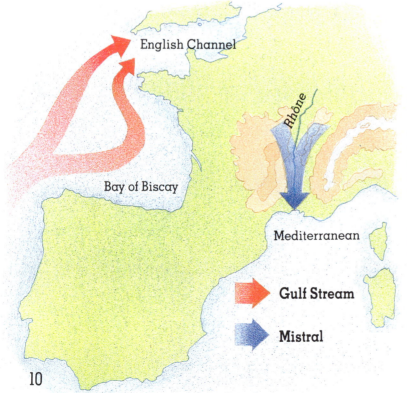

English Channel

Rhône

Bay of Biscay

Mediterranean

Gulf Stream

Mistral

The Gulf Stream
The ocean current called the Gulf Stream brings warm water from the tropical Atlantic. It flows along the west coast of France, making the climate here mild and damp all year.

A fearsome wind
In the east the *Mistral*, a fierce, cold wind, blows in the winter down the Rhône Valley from the Massif Central. It is much feared by local farmers since it can destroy crops and blow down trees and buildings.

Holiday paradise

Along the south coast, shielded by the Maritime Alps, is the narrow lush strip of the French Riviera – the Côte d'Azur ("sky-blue coast"). The weather is hot and sunny in summer, warm and bright in winter. People come to this famous resort area from all over the world.

Skiing in springtime

On the higher peaks of the Alps the snow covers the ground well into spring. Resorts such as Chamonix and Val d'Izère are packed with skiers and sightseers.

FLAMINGOES AND COWBOYS

Lying at the heart of Western Europe, France shares its wildlife with the countries around it. There is an enormous variety of animals and plants. On the wild, rugged coasts of the northwest are the huge seabird colonies at Cap Fréhel and Cap Sizun. In the south the land is dry and dusty, with exotic birds like flamingoes and hoopoes.

Along France's west coast are large areas of salt marshes, lagoons, and bogs. Each year thousands upon thousands of water birds spend the winter here, or rest for a few days on their migrations between Northern Europe and Africa.

In ancient times much of the country was covered by thick forests. Over the years these have largely been cut down to make way for farmland, houses, and factories. Even so, there are still big forests of oak, chestnut, beech, and pine to the south of the Massif Central and on the slopes of the Alps and Pyrenees. These forests are the homes of eagles, vultures, wild cats, and wild boars.

Cowboy country

In the south, as the Rhône River flows into the Mediterranean, it spreads out into a vast delta. This is the Camargue, one of the biggest areas of marshland in Europe. More than 300 kinds of birds live here, including the greater flamingo, as well as black bulls and half-wild white horses like those below. The horses and bulls are looked after by French *guardians*, who live in much the same way as did the cowboys in the wild west of America.

Greater flamingo

Shoot or protect?
Hunting, and especially
shooting, have always been
popular in France. Until
recently the French have not
done much in the way of nature
conservation. However, there
are now more than 100 nature
reserves and national parks,
and many mammals and all
birds of prey (hawks, eagles,
and owls) are protected by law.

Red-crested pochard

Hoopoe

Wild boar

Wild cat

Ibex

Lady's slipper orchid

Lizard orchid

13

DOWN ON THE FARM

Farming and fishing have always been major sources of jobs and money for the French. Almost one-third of the country is cultivated, and one-quarter of this is pasture land for animals. France produces more cereals, meat, poultry, cheese, and sugar than any other country in Europe. Farm goods make up one-fifth of French exports.

The richest pastures are around Paris and in the north and west. Sheep and goats are herded mainly on the lower slopes of the Alps and Pyrenees. Pigs are raised in Britanny, and horses to the north of the Massif Central. There are poultry farms across the country. Potatoes come from Britanny, tobacco grows in the southwest, rice in the southeast, and fruit all over the south. Grapes and apples are the most important fruits, the grapes being used to make world-famous French wines.

One-quarter of France is covered with forests. New trees are planted to replace those that are cut down. The timber is used for paper, building, and furniture.

KEY FACTS

▶ The French eat more cheese and drink more wine, on average, than any other nation.
▶ A bottle of Rémy Martin *Louis XIII* cognac (a kind of brandy) would cost most people two weeks' wages.
▶ Le Leruns, a French cheese made from goat's milk, is probably the most expensive cheese in the world.
▶ The largest vineyard on earth is in the south of France. It covers more than 1,977,000 acres.

Wine and cheese, please

The French make more than 250 kinds of wine and 240 different cheeses. Lovers of good food and drink say there are none better. Among the famous French wines are Champagne, Bordeaux, Beaujolais, and Burgundy. Cheeses are made from cow, goat, and ewe milk. They include Camembert, Roquefort, and Brie.

Big is efficient

In recent years the pattern of French farming has changed. Small family holdings, like those dotting the landscape in the picture above, have given way to huge, modern, high-technology farms, and the number of farm workers has dropped dramatically. This is largely the result of the EEC which pays farmers high prices for goods no matter how much they produce.

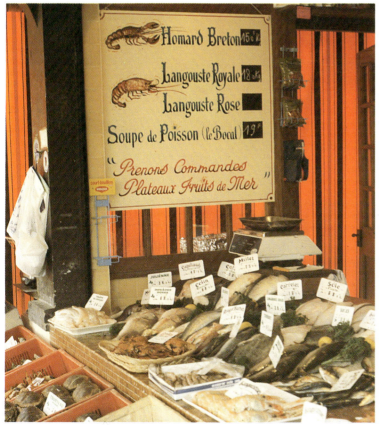

Fresh French fish

France's fishing industry is growing. There are more than 75,000 fishermen using 10,000 ships. Each year they harvest 700,000 tons of fish and shellfish from the seas. Boulogne is the main fishing port.

FACTORIES AND INDUSTRIES

Many of the products of French industry are world famous. Cars by Citroën, Renault, and Peugeot, equipped with Michelin tires; Limoges porcelain and pottery; Thompson computers; and the TGV train are some of the best-known names. Today France is fourth in the list of exporters, after America, West Germany, and Japan. More than half of foreign trade is with the EEC, but America and the Middle East are also major customers.

After World War II, France quickly built up its iron, steel, and energy industries. The country has large supplies of coal, iron ore, bauxite (aluminum ore), sulphur oil, and natural gas. With these the nation's factories turn out cars, trucks, ships, machinery, plastics, fertilizers, textiles, glassware, and household goods.

France now has the twelfth-highest standard of living in the world. French industry has modernized its factories and uses the latest technology. Even so, like other major nations, there have been problems in recent years. Of a working population of 21 million people, two million have no jobs.

The tourist trade

More people go on vacations to France than anywhere else in Europe. They come to see the historic *châteaux* (great castles), ancient cities, beautiful countryside and marvelous coastline, and sample the food and wine. Château d'Yquem in Bordeaux, shown here, is famed for its Sauternes wine. Tourism provides hundreds of thousands of jobs. Foreign visitors spend a sum equal to one-fourteenth of the value of France's exports.

The nuclear age

Industry needs energy. France's own supplies of coal and natural gas are decreasing, and the cost of oil is rising. So the country has developed its nuclear energy. Nuclear power stations like this one now provide almost one-quarter of France's energy.

New forms of energy

In France there is much research into two new sources of energy. One is heat and light from the sun. At Odeillo, in the Pyrenees, the "solar furnace" shown here was built in 1970, and another is planned.

The second source of energy is the rise and fall of sea water with the tides. At the mouth of the Rance River, in Britanny, water flows through turbines that turn tidal power into electricity.

FRANCE ON THE MOVE

The French have one of the best transportation systems of any country. Much of the land is flat, and roads and railways, rivers and canals criss-cross the country and carry people and freight quickly and safely.

SNCF, France's national railway, is the envy of the world. There are nearly 22,000 miles of tracks and the trains are fast, clean, and on time. Four trains out of five are electric. The railways transport about three-quarters of all people and freight in France. There are few long-distance buses because the trains are so good.

Countless tourists travel across Europe on France's 4,000 miles of *autoroutes* (highways). Many sections charge a toll and the money goes to the upkeep of the roads. In the eastern half of the country, canals and rivers carry huge amounts of freight between industrial cities like Paris, Strasbourg, and Rouen, and to the international ports of Marseille, Le Havre, and Calais.

Highest-speed train
France is very proud of its national railway, the SNCF (Société Nationale des Chemins de Fer). The TGV or *Train à Grande Vitesse* ("Very Fast Train") runs the fastest regular service in the world. It can reach an incredible 235 miles per hour. The trip from Paris to Lyon, 300 miles, takes just two hours.

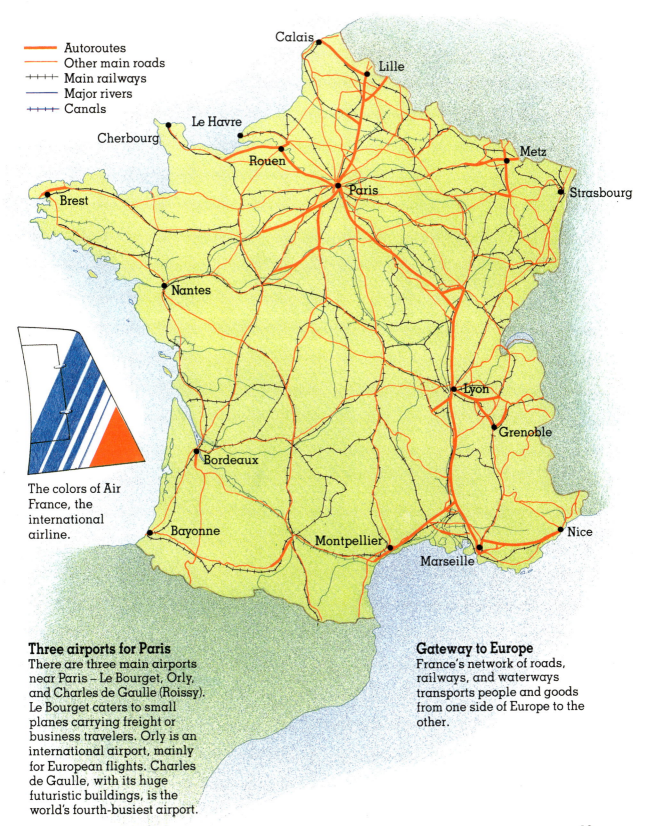

Autoroutes
Other main roads
+++++ **Main railways**
Major rivers
+++++ **Canals**

Calais

Lille

Cherbourg
Le Havre
Rouen
Paris
Metz
Strasbourg

Brest

Nantes

Lyon

Grenoble

Bordeaux

Bayonne

Montpellier

Marseille

Nice

The colors of Air France, the international airline.

Three airports for Paris

There are three main airports near Paris – Le Bourget, Orly, and Charles de Gaulle (Roissy). Le Bourget caters to small planes carrying freight or business travelers. Orly is an international airport, mainly for European flights. Charles de Gaulle, with its huge futuristic buildings, is the world's fourth-busiest airport.

Gateway to Europe

France's network of roads, railways, and waterways transports people and goods from one side of Europe to the other.

19

BON APPETIT!

Breakfast

This is simple and quick. It is usually a cup of coffee, or perhaps chocolate milk, with bread (French, of course) and butter and maybe jam, or croissants.

France is well known for its good cooking, fine wines, and superb restaurants. For many families, the main meal is the most important part of the day. The French talk endlessly about food and drink.

What makes French cooking so good? Part of the skill is to buy good ingredients. French cooks are very fussy about what they choose to go into a dish. To bring out the flavors they use garlic and other spices. They take great care in preparing, cooking, and serving as well. The French regard food as something to linger over and enjoy, not to be gulped down quickly before doing something else.

Meals served in good restaurants or for special occasions at home may have four or five courses and last several hours. Children are encouraged to go with their parents to restaurants, take an interest in their food, and carry on this great French tradition.

KEY FACTS

Remember the following when you "eat French":
▶ Wine is the standard drink, even for children but for them it is usually mixed with water.
▶ The fork is put on the table with the prongs facing downward.
▶ Don't leave your cutlery on the plate after eating your appetizer – you keep the same knife and fork throughout the meal.
▶ Many people do not drink tap water but prefer mineral water from bottles, either fizzy (*gazeuse*) or still (*non-gazeuse*).
▶ Coffee is drunk much more often than tea, but many people will not drink coffee at night for it might keep them awake.

The pavement café
The typical French café or restaurant has tables and chairs outside, on the pavement. People sit in the sunshine and enjoy a glass of wine or a full five-course meal.

Wine in the making
Wine-making is a major industry in many parts of France. Grapes ripen in the sun and are then taken to the presses by tractor and trailer.

Special dishes of the regions
In the south *bouillabaisse* is a popular dish. It is a fish stew that includes a mixture of eels, monkfish, lobsters, crabs, and mussels. In the southwest people like *cassoulet*, a meat stew made with slices of sausage, bacon or goose, pork and white beans. A speciality of the southeast is *pissaladière*, a pastry tart with onions, tomatoes, anchovies, and spices.

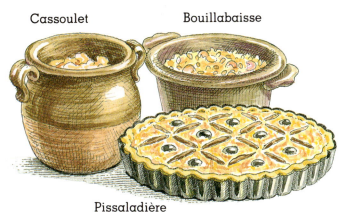

Cassoulet

Bouillabaisse

Pissaladière

CENTER FOR THE ARTS

France has certainly produced great buildings, works of art, writers, and musicians. The Romans constructed enormous amphitheaters at Nîmes and Arles. During the Middle Ages, great cathedrals were built such as Notre-Dame in Paris, Chartres, and Reims.

During the 15th and 16th centuries the artistic Renaissance spread from neighboring Italy. It started slowly in France, but by the 18th century Paris was the cultural center of Europe. Great French writers include Rabelais, La Fontaine, Molière, and Voltaire. Their works are still admired as some of the greatest ever written, reflecting the politics and troubled moods of their times.

In recent years France continues to produce great artists and musicians. They include the philosophers and writers Jean-Paul Sartre and Albert Camus, the painter Marc Chagall, the composers Debussy, Ravel, and Massiaen, and the world's leading mime artist, Marcel Marceau.

Fun and games
The Romans built huge amphitheaters in the south of France, in towns such as Nîmes, Orange, and Arles. They held "games" where warriors would fight each other or wild animals to the death. Today the amphitheaters are used for rock concerts, theatrical plays, and French bull-fighting. The bull is not harmed; the idea is to pull colored tassels from its horns.

The Impressionists

One of France's greatest gifts to the art world has been the "Impressionist" style of painting, developed in the late 19th century. Impressionists did not try to paint exactly what they saw. Instead they changed the colors and the effects of light in their works, to create an "impression" of their subject. Great French Impressionists include Manet, Monet, Degas, Renoir, and Cézanne.

Figures in metal and marble

Auguste Rodin was one of the greatest sculptors of the last century. He was brought up in Paris, and studied medicine as well as sculpture, so that he could model the human body so perfectly. His most famous works include *Age of Bronze* and *The Thinker* (shown here).

A medieval masterpiece

Chartres Cathedral (*Notre-Dame de Chartres*) towers above the town of Chartres, 56 miles southwest of Paris. The cathedral was built between 1194 and 1220, and it is regarded as one of the most magnificent medieval buildings in the world. Many experts say that the stained glass in its 200 windows is the finest dating from that period.

PARIS, CITY OF LIGHT

Paris is one of the most beautiful and romantic cities in the world. It attracts visitors from all corners of the globe, who come to visit such well-known places as the Eiffel Tower, the Louvre art galleries, Notre-Dame cathedral, and Sacré-Coeur church. There are elegant *boulevards* (avenues), bustling shops selling the best in food and fashion, quiet parks, sidewalk cafés, and an active night-life.

Paris has grown steadily through its history. During the Middle Ages it became a center of culture and learning, and the brightest students came to its university, the Sorbonne. Each French king ordered the building of new palaces, churches, and museums, to leave his mark on the city. People flocked to the city in search of work and wealth.

The historic center of Paris is quite small – you can walk across it in an hour. But the Paris region spreads for many miles, with office buildings, factories, and high-rise apartments dotting the horizon. On the outskirts are modern housing projects. Nearly 10 million people live in and near the city, making Paris the world's sixth-largest built-up area.

Arc de Triomphe

This great arch, 164 feet high, was ordered by Napoleon to celebrate his victories. It was completed in 1836.

Arc de Triomphe

Eiffel Tower

Pompidou Center

This strange new building is a museum of modern art, exhibition center and library. The pipes, tubes, cables and ducts are not hidden in the walls, as is usual, but are on the outskirts and are brightly painted.

Sacré-Coeur

Montmartre
With the Pigalle district, this is the center for night clubs, theaters and restaurants. On its hill is Sacré-Coeur church.

• Sacré-Coeur

Pigalle

Shops and stores
On and around the Avenue des Champs-Elysées are world-famous stores and hotels, and the fashion and cosmetic houses such as Yves Saint-Laurent, Christian Dior, and Ted Lapidus.

Arc de Triomphe
•

Champs-Elysées

Bourse
•

Louvre Les Halles
• • • Pompidou Center

Seine River
• Eiffel
Tower

Ile de la Cité
•

Les Halles
For 800 years this was the city's food market. Now new glass and concrete buildings make up the Forum, a complex of shops, leisure centers, and halls for sports and exhibitions. Next to the Forum is a children's "fun palace" where grown-ups are not allowed!

The Right Bank
This is the business center, with the *Bourse* (Paris Stock Exchange) and the head offices of banks and big companies.

•
Sorbonne

Right
Bank

The Latin Quarter
With the University at its center, this students' district has narrow, old streets full of colorful cafés and bars.

Left
Bank

The Left Bank
Many artists, writers, and crafts people live in this area. Some of the world's greatest paintings came from here.

Notre-Dame

Ile de la Cité
This boat-shaped island in the River Seine is the city's historic heart. Notre-Dame cathedral was finished here in 1345.

FROM THE GAULS TO THE SUN KING

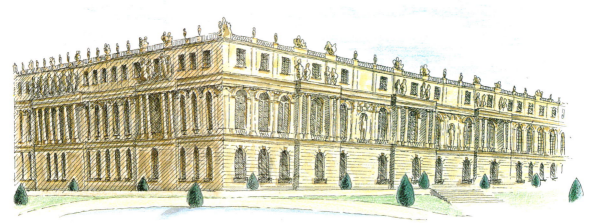

In ancient times, Celtic tribes lived in the area we now call France. Then, in 59 BC, the Romans marched through France and in a few years had conquered it. They built towns, roads, and great amphitheaters, and they brought with them new methods of farming.

As the Roman Empire began to topple in the 5th century, several tribes from Germany and Scandinavia invaded France. The Frankish chief, Clovis, brought the tribes under control at the end of the 5th century, and the Franks ruled for 400 years.

By the late 10th century Norsemen from Denmark and Norway had invaded the area of Normandy. They took power away from the kings and gave it to the lords and barons. All over France, great castles were built to keep out invaders. Then, from 1337 to 1453, France and England fought a long series of battles. The English controlled the western half of the country. But by the 17th century they had been driven out and the time of the great French kings had begun. The greatest of these kings was Louis XIV, known as the "Sun King" because he believed that he was the "sun" that lit up the nation.

Home fit for a king
One of the most magnificent palaces in Europe is the Palace of Versailles, about 12 miles southwest of Paris. It was built for Louis XIV between 1666 and 1700, to show his greatness and to house his nobles and government officials. At the height of his reign more than 1,000 courtiers, 4,000 servants, and 10,000 officials lived or worked at Versailles.

Savior or witch?

In 1429, during the "Hundred Years War" with England, the town of Orleans was surrounded. Joan of Arc, a farmer's daughter, convinced the king that she was inspired by God to help France. Led by her, the French army broke the eight-month English siege. In 1430 Joan tried to help recapture Paris but she was captured by the English and turned over to a French church court. After months of questioning she was tricked into admitting she was a witch. She was burned at the stake in 1431, at Rouen. Today she is a national heroine and saint.

Charles the Great

The most important Frankish king of France was Charlemagne, whose statue you can see above. He lived from 742 to 814 and made France the center of an empire that included Germany and Italy. He also encouraged artists and scholars, laying the foundations for France to become the cultural center of Europe.

 Extent of Charlemagne's Empire

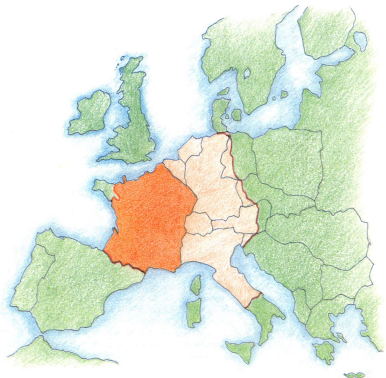

LONG LIVE THE REVOLUTION!

After the death of the glorious Louis XIV in 1715, the power of France slowly faded. Louis' successor, Louis XV, had many problems. He was defeated in wars abroad, while at home many people were poor and had little to eat. There was much unrest in the country.

In July 1789 the people's anger burst out. They stormed the Bastille, the prison in Paris. The revolution began and the new king, Louis XVI, was overthrown. In 1792, after much bloodshed, France became a republic. This meant that power was in the hands of the people. The new government introduced *The Declaration of the Rights of Man* with the famous words: liberty, equality, fraternity.

There followed a year-long Reign of Terror when the flashing blade of the guillotine was rarely still. Among those beheaded were the king, his wife Marie Antoinette, thousands of noblemen and others who were considered traitors to the state. Then the new leaders began to fight among themselves until, in 1804, Napoleon made himself Emperor of France.

The Bastille stormed

The French Revolution began on July 14, 1789 when a mob attacked the Bastille. Many political prisoners were held in this grim fortress. The angry crowd killed the guards, freed the prisoners, and destroyed the whole area. Ever since, people all over France have celebrated Bastille Day with fireworks, parties, dancing in the streets, and military parades. This painting by Eugène Delacroix (1830) shows the spirit of the revolution. It is called *Liberty Leading the People*.

The French Empire

During the Napoleonic wars (1803-1814) France waged battles against Austria, Prussia, and Russia. By 1812 Napoleon controlled all of Western Europe and some of Eastern Europe as well.

- France
- Countries controlled by Napoleon
- Free countries

Russia

Battle of Waterloo

Prussia

Battle of Austerlitz

France

Austria

Battle of Trafalgar

28

The little general
Napoleon Bonaparte was a brilliant soldier in the French army. In 1794, aged only 25, he became a general. In 1799 he made himself First Consul of France. After he became emperor in 1804, his navy was beaten by the English fleet under Nelson, at the Battle of Trafalgar. This stopped the French from invading England. After his downfall, Napoleon was sent to the island of St. Helena, where he died in 1821. His remains were taken to the Hôtel des Invalides in Paris, which is now a national shrine.

Off with their heads!
The guillotine was the weapon of the people during the revolution. It was invented by a doctor named Joseph Guillotin. He wanted condemned people to suffer as little pain as possible on execution.

29

ONE NATION AT LAST

About 400 years ago, France was made up of separate provinces and kingdoms. This was the result of land being divided up after many wars, treaties, and royal marriages. There was no overall ruler.

The French kings and, in the 1800s, Napoleon Bonaparte tried to bring the provinces under the control of the capital, Paris. Napoleon divided the country into 90 *départements*. Each *département* had a main town with a prefect (a sort of mayor) and a smaller town with a sub-prefect. The prefects were under the control of officials in Paris.

Napoleon developed a strong system of government. But wealth and power became centered in Paris and the north. In recent years the government has tried to spread wealth and power more evenly. Today France is divided into 22 regions, which are split into 96 *départements*. Each region is governed by a Regional Council that is elected by the local people. Even so, in many ways the country is still run from Paris.

The Parisian way

Paris has been the center of French government and culture for centuries. Although this is slowly changing, many Parisians (people from Paris) still think themselves superior to the "provincials," as people from the countryside are known. Some Parisians even regard the rest of France as a "desert," lacking in money, jobs, and culture. There is a great contrast between life on a country farm and the sophisticated ways of Parisian café society.

The three Michaels

Many Breton people, from Brittany in the northwest of France, are descended from Celts, who were driven out of Cornwall, England, by the Romans in the 5th century. The Bretons still have cultural links with their Celtic cousins in Cornwall, Wales, and Ireland. Three places named in honor of Saint Michael are important in Celtic folklore.

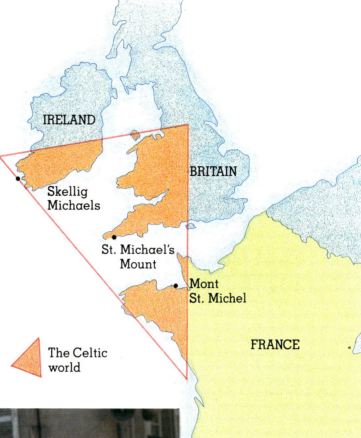

IRELAND

BRITAIN

Skellig Michaels

St. Michael's Mount

Mont St. Michel

FRANCE

The Celtic world

Country costumes

Although France is now one nation, people from the various regions are proud of their own history. They keep their past alive with feasts and celebrations, and with local costumes like those worn by the Breton women shown here.

31

FRANCE IN THE 20th CENTURY

After Napoleon's time, kings ruled France once again. But during the 19th century the French did not progress as quickly as their neighbors Britain and Germany, who were growing in military and industrial strength. In 1871, after defeat by the Prussians, another French republic was set up. This time there was a strong government and the country gained wealth from its own industrial revolution and its colonies abroad. French fortunes were improving.

Then came the two world wars. France became the main battlefield. In World War I more than one million French soldiers died and two million were injured. During World War II the Free French Army (the "Résistance") kept up an underground war against the occupying Germans. When Free French, British, and American troops freed the country in 1945, the French people were exhausted and the country was in chaos.

It was only in 1958 when General de Gaulle set up the fifth Republic, that stability returned. Within a few years the economy was on the mend and France had become a great power once again.

France in space

Ariane is a rocket designed and built by several European countries, with France leading the way. It launches satellites and other space craft. After the Shuttle Challenger disaster in 1986, *Ariane* took the lead in space research.

Ariane rocket

World's fastest airliner

France is a world leader in technology and engineering. The supersonic Concorde airliner was built by French and British companies. It went into service in 1976, carrying 130 passengers at 1,300 miles per hour.

Concorde

The seat of Government

The French "parliament" sits at La Chambre des Députés, in Paris. There are two sets of elected members, the Senate (295 members) and the National Assembly (491 members). Everyone aged 18 and over can vote.

Charles de Gaulle

De Gaulle led the French through World War II. In 1946 he resigned because he did not agree with the rules of the new republic. Then in 1958 there was a crisis over independence for Algeria, a French colony in North Africa. France was threatened with civil war. De Gaulle was elected president. He negotiated with the Algerians, allowing them to vote on whether they wanted independence. They did, and Algeria became independent in 1962. De Gaulle finally retired in 1969 and died in 1970. His policies have affected all aspects of French life.

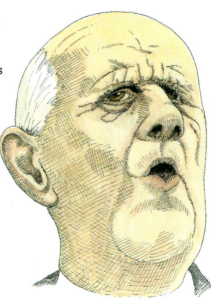

KEY FACTS

▶ The only bank that can make new French banknotes is the Banque de France, founded by Napoleon in 1800.

▶ There are more than 500,000 people in the French army, navy, and air force. Every man has to spend 12 months doing military service.

▶ Over one-quarter of France's 20 million workers are in manufacturing jobs.

▶ On May 1 each year there are official celebrations for "Labor Day."

NEWS AND COMMUNICATIONS

France has three main television channels: TF1, A2, and FR3. They get their money mainly from advertising. There are also many cable and satellite channels, which show mostly films. The quality of French television is not especially high. Some of the most popular programs are from Britain and America, with subtitles or French voices added.

There are also three main radio stations. France Inter is for news, music, and plays, France Culture specializes in educational and cultural programs. France Musique plays classical music. Listeners can also receive programs such as Radio Luxembourg and Europe Number 1 from West Germany. These radio stations broadcast mainly rock music.

French people like to read newspapers and books. There are more than 80 papers published each day, mainly local ones. News magazines and special interest magazines are becoming more popular, on subjects like fashion, cars, food, wine, and sports.

Phone home...

Many homes have the modern French telephone system, *Minitel*. Each phone is like a small computer linked into the main network. To find someone's phone number, you call the central computer and type in the person's name – and their address and phone number appear on your *Minitel* screen. You can also call recorded reports on the news, weather, road, and rail services.

TV from the sky

France is at the center of Europe so people can receive many television programs from neighboring countries. They are also well placed for satellite broadcasts. Some parts of France can pick up over 20 television channels, playing everything from old films to all-day music videos.

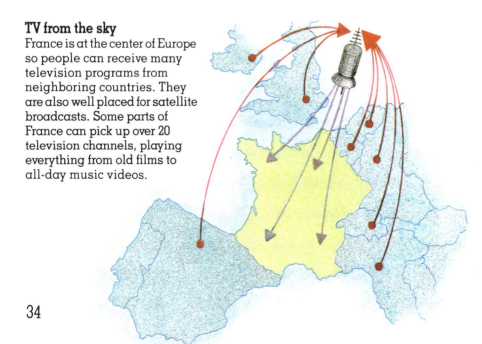

The daily paper

Three out of five French adults read at least one newspaper every day. Newspapers are a very popular form of communication. Compared to other countries, the French prefer to read about events rather than watch them on the news.

News of the world

French newsstands are full of papers and magazines. The best-known national newspapers are *Le Monde* ("The World"), *Le Figaro*, and *France-Soir*. However, regional papers such as *Ouest-France* and *Le Progrès* sell more copies.

KEY FACTS

▶ The *Astérix* and *Tintin* children's comic books have been translated into every major language in the world.
▶ Almost every family in France has a set of *Le Petit Larousse*, a combined picture encyclopedia and dictionary.
▶ The best-selling magazine in France is *Télé 7 Jours*, the weekly guide to television programs. It sells more than three million copies every week.

AT HOME WITH THE FAMILY

Family life is very important to the French. Compared to other countries, the average French family spends a lot of time together. They eat their meals, go on vacation, and pass much of their spare time together. Parents like to be with their children, but they encourage the children to show respect and be independent.

Many French children stay up quite late in the evenings, talking over dinner, reading, or watching television. They are expected to help with household chores such as setting and clearing the table, and washing dishes. In most homes, the father is the head of the family but the mother is the center of family life.

As teenagers grow up, they tend to live at home longer than in other countries. After graduation they live with their parents until they have been working for a few years or until they get married. Most students go to a local university or college and stay at home, rather than moving away and living in a dorm or renting an apartment.

More children

In recent years the number of French people has increased only slightly. As a nation, France once considered that its population was too small. So the government provided money in the form of child allowances to encourage parents to have more than one child. Mothers can also now go out to work and leave their children in day-care centers partly paid for by the state. Women and men in the same job must be paid the same – by law.

Down at the café

Many young French people meet in their local cafés for a cup of coffee and a chat. They are eager to take part in the traditional French "art" of conversation.

Two marriages

The traditional French marriage is in two parts. The first is the civil ceremony at the local town hall, where the couple signs the legal contract in front of the mayor. The second is the religious ceremony. This usually takes place right after the civil part and consists of a wedding service in church.

KEY FACTS

▶ Many French children have a first name that is made up of two names, such as *Jean-Paul* or *Marie-Louise*. One of the names is that of a saint.

▶ And most French children have two birthdays! One is the anniversary of the day they were born. The other is the "birthday" of the saint they were named after. (Each day in the year is dedicated to a saint.)

▶ In France, New Years, rather than Christmas, is the time for giving presents and visiting friends and relations.

▶ The average age for getting married is 23 for women and 25 for men.

▶ The average age that French people live to is 78 for women and 70 for men.

OFF TO SHOP

The main street of the average French town has the same kinds of stores you would find in most countries. The butcher, bakery, fish store and drug store are easy to recognize. But there are a few distinctly French shops – you can see one opposite.

In the cities and towns, many people prefer to shop in their local main street rather than travel to a supermarket. They usually know the shopkeepers and enjoy a chat with them. A typical family shops each day for bread, fruit and vegetables, meat, and milk. Food stores open early, about 7:30am, and close about 8pm, so that people can shop before or after work. They close for at least two hours in the middle of the day, for a leisurely lunch.

In smaller towns and villages people tend to shop at the market. This is usually held in the village square. Local traders, farmers and businesses set up their stalls on market day. In the middle of the square there is often a covered hall for the butcher, fish seller, and baker.

Some typically French shops

Crémerie A sort of milk shop that sells dairy foods – cream, butter, eggs, and milk.
Charcuterie A specialized pork butcher and delicatessen that sells pork meats, cooked meats, and quality cold-cut meats like salami.
Patisserie A special kind of baker who sells pastries, cakes, and sweet breads such as the famous, flaky, crescent-shaped *croissant* rolls.
Bar-Tabac A bar selling not only beer, wine, and other alcoholic drinks, but also coffee, snacks, cigarettes, tobacco, and postage stamps, and even bus and train tickets. Many French people have their lunch here. Look for the cigar-shaped sign outside.

The hypermarket

France was one of the first European countries to copy the American idea of having giant supermarkets on the outskirts of towns, where you can buy almost anything. The slogan on the side of this one means "Everything for the home". The hypermarket near Marseille is Europe's largest, covering the area of four soccer fields.

Home of good food

French food looks delicious even when it's just on display in the shop. Great care is taken to keep fresh, tasty ingredients for the shoppers.

Meet you at the market

The local market is as much a place for talking as it is for shopping. Farmers discuss the weather or the price of beef, while shoppers meet in the café for a coffee and chat.

A DAY AT SCHOOL

In a typical French school, the day begins at 8:30am. There are two lessons, followed by a short break, then another two lessons. The two-hour midday break begins at 12:30pm. Some children go home while others have a meal at school. The afternoon starts at 2:30pm and there are three lessons, lasting until 5:30pm.

This might seem like a long day. But most French children do not go to school at all on Wednesdays, though they do have lessons on Saturday morning. At many schools there is no official uniform to wear. Older children have homework every day. School vacations last for only a few days at Christmas and Easter. However, summer vacations are up to 10 weeks long.

In the classroom

The average French class has up to 40 pupils. Each lesson lasts 55 minutes. It begins with *le professeur* (the teacher) asking a few children some questions to see how much they have learned. In general, lessons are quite formal: the teacher talks, the pupils listen and learn. There are also school outings, when the children learn about the historic buildings, parks, and gardens of their country.

Kindergarten

Three children out of five between the ages of 2 and 4 go to nursery school, day-care, or kindergarten.

Primary school

All children must attend between the ages of 6 and 11. The main lessons are reading, writing, and mathematics, with history, geography, and science for the older children.

Secondary school

Children aged between 11 and 16 go to secondary school. Everyone does the same subjects until aged 14. Then they can choose an "academic" course which hopefully leads to university or college, or a "vocational" course that prepares them for a trade or craft.

The "bac"

The *baccalauréat* is an exam taken around the age of 18. Students choose one of five main courses: literature, economics, technology, science, or math. They take 11 separate subjects and their marks are averaged to see if they pass. If they fail, they can take the exam again. Passing the "bac" means you have the right to go to a university or college.

Famous French writers

The writing teacher

Jean-Paul Sartre is one of the greatest writers of our century. He was a teacher in Paris until 1945, then he became a full-time author of novels, plays and philosophical works.

The fourth musketeer

Alexandre Dumas, who lived during the middle of the 19th century, wrote exciting novels such as *The Three Musketeers* and *The Count of Monte Cristo.*

I am, I think...

René Descartes was a brilliant 17th-century mathematician and philosopher. He wrote the famous words: "I think, therefore I am." (Actually it was *Cogito, ergo sum,* since he wrote in Latin.)

41

THE SPORTING FRENCH

French people spend half their spare time, on average, reading or going to the movies, theater, or concert hall. For most of them, however, the main pastime is going to a restaurant or café and having a meal or drinks with friends.

Many French families have a month's vacation in the summer, either July or August. On the first days of these months the roads and trains are crowded with people going off to the coast, vacationing and camping. The beaches, especially in the south, get very crowded. August is a good month for foreign visitors to see Paris in peace and quiet, since almost all Parisians are away.

Some French people, especially parents with young children, like to take a winter vacation instead. They relax or ski in the mountains. Schools organize many vacations for their pupils. In the winter school children go skiing and skating. In the summer they explore the arts, crafts, nature, history, and great buildings of their country.

Great sporting events

① The *Tour de France*, the world's leading cycle race, is 2,982 miles long. Each year it has a new route around the country.

② The French Open is one of the top four tennis tournaments, with Wimbledon and the U.S. and Australian Opens.

③ The Monte Carlo Rally for production cars has starting points all over Europe. It finishes at Monte Carlo, the tourist center of Monaco.

④ *Prix de l'Arc de Triomphe*, one of the world's great horse races, is run at the Longchamps course near Paris.

⑤ In the *Le Mans 24-hour*, sports cars race all day and night at speeds of up to 250 miles per hour.

Hitting the jack

Probably the most popular sport in France is *boules*, which is similar to bowls in Britain. It can be played on any flat open space, particularly the sandy tracks in parks and town squares. Each player has two metal balls which he throws and tries to hit a smaller ball, the jack. The person whose ball lands nearest the jack is the winner.

Monte Carlo here we come

The bright lights of Monte Carlo attract many tourists from all over Europe. This seaside resort is in Monaco, a small country on France's southern coast. It is famous for its casinos, fine beaches, and as the finish of the Monte Carlo Rally.

TOMORROW'S FRANCE

The world oil crisis in the 1970s affected France in the same way as many other rich countries. People were put out of work, and the prices of gasoline, oil, and many goods went up fast. Yet through determination and hard work the French people pulled through. The country's industries and economy have recovered well compared to many other nations. France is likely to continue as the leading nation in the EEC. Overseas trade with the United States, Eastern Europe, and the Middle East is on the increase.

France has always been proud of its independence in the world. The French are not afraid to "go it alone" in areas such as nuclear power, weapons research, and aerospace research. And France wants to keep on good terms both with the Western countries and with the Soviet Union and its Eastern allies. The France of the future is likely to be a strong, capable, and independent nation.

The "Chunnel"

In 1986 the French and English agreed to build a tunnel under the English Channel. Two railway lines will carry passengers, cars, trucks, and freight. There will also be small service tunnels. France hopes that the Channel Tunnel or "Chunnel" will bring in extra tourists and business people, especially to the north of the country where economic problems have hit hardest.

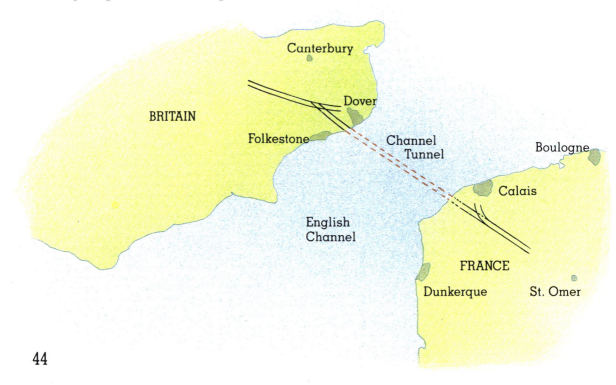

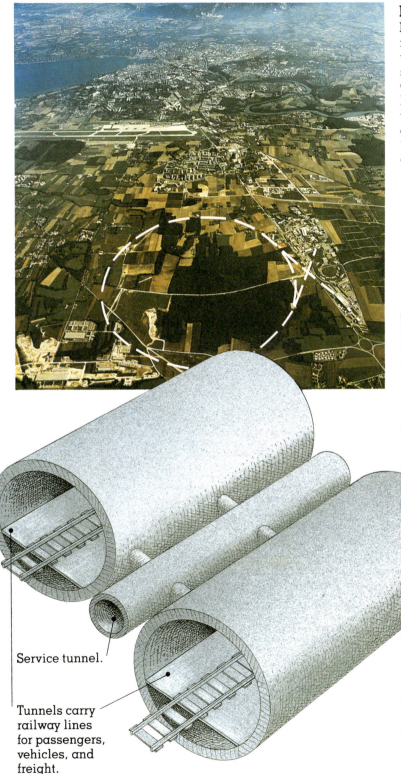

Eureka!

Ever anxious to lead in scientific research, France is joining forces with other European countries such as Britain and West Germany. This is the *Euréka* Project (named after the words of the mathematician Archimedes as he sat in the tub and meaning "I've found it!") The European group will compete with Japan and the United States in areas such as atomic physics, robots, and aircraft design. Here you can see the site of an underground Super-Proton-Synchrotron accelerator – where the particles of atoms are studied.

Service tunnel.

Tunnels carry railway lines for passengers, vehicles, and freight.

KEY FACTS

▶ More than 30 countries around the world used to be under the control of France, in the old French Empire. Now there are only 10, mostly small islands.

▶ The French are in the forefront of medical research for serious diseases such as AIDS.

▶ The French are building more nuclear power stations than any other country in Europe. Their safety record for nuclear power is one of the best in the world.

▶ By 1990 there should be high-speed TGV trains running between all main French cities.

▶ France's own version of the space shuttle, *Hermes*, could be built before the year 2000.

Index

Acknowledgments
All illustrations by Ann Savage.
Photographic credits (*a* = above, *b* = below, *m* = middle, *l* = left, *r* = right):
Cover *al* Centre Audiovisual SNCF, *bl* Klaus Kerth/Zefa, *ar* Zefa, *br* Dr H Wirth/Zefa; page 8 Renault Ltd; page 9 BPCC/Aldus Archive; page 11 *a* Chris Forsey, *b* Chastel/French Government Tourist Office; page 12 Zefa; page 15 *a* Klaus Kerth/Zefa, *b* Chancerel Publishers; page 17 Alex Bartel/Science Photo Library; page 18 Centre Audiovisual SNCF; page 21 *a* Bernard Regent/Hutchinson Library, *b* Michael Busselle; page 22 Chancerel Publishers; page 23 Chris Forsey; page 24 Lionel Bender; page 27 Weidenfeld and Nicolson Ltd; page 29 Louvre/Bridgeman Art Library; page 30 Michael Busselle (woman), Damm/Zefa (Paris); page 31 Dr H Wirth/Zefa; page 33 Spectrum Colour Library; page 35 *a* Chancerel Publishers, *b* Michael Busselle; page 36 Chancerel Publishers; page 37 Robert Cundy/Robert Harding Picture Library; page 38 Chancerel Publishers; page 39 *al* Chancerel Publishers, *ar* Lionel Bender, *b* Chancerel Publishers; page 40 Michael H Black/Robert Harding Picture Library; page 43 *a* Chancerel Publishers, *b* Lionel Bender; page 45 Science Photo Library.